Family Fun

T0025643

Healthy Living

This is my family.
I stay healthy
with my family.

Nan and Pop

Mom

Dad

My sister

Me

I play soccer

with my mom and dad.

I can run fast.

I throw the Frisbee with my dad.

I can throw the Frisbee up.

Up, up, up!

I go for a walk

with my family.

We walk and walk.

Look at us.

We can walk a long way.